D0983911

AFTERNOON
OF A
PAWNBROKER

By the Same Author

POETRY

POEMS

ANGEL ARMS

DEAD RECKONING

COLLECTED POEMS

NOVELS

THE HOSPITAL

DAGGER OF THE MIND

CLARK GIFFORD'S BODY

AFTERNOON OF A PAWNBROKER

and other poems

by

KENNETH FEARING

NEW YORK
HARCOURT, BRACE AND COMPANY

first edition

PRINTED IN THE UNITED STATES OF AMERICA

TO ELIZABETH AMES

Thanks are due to the *New Yorker,* the *New Republic, Poetry Magazine,* the *Partisan Review,* the James M. Decker Press, and *American Anthology,* for their kind permission to reprint poems in this book.

CONTENTS

AFTERNOON OF A PAWNBROKER

CONTINUOUS PERFORMANCE

The place seems strange, more strange than ever, and the times are still more out of joint;
Perhaps there has been some slight mistake?

It is like arriving at the movies late, as usual, just as the story ends:
There is a carnival on the screen. It is a village in springtime, that much is clear. But why has the heroine suddenly slapped his face? And what does it mean, the sequence with the limousine and the packed valise? Very strange.
Then love wins. Fine. And it is the end. O.K.
But how do we reach that carnival again? And when will that springtime we saw return once more? How, and when?

Now, where a moment ago there was a village square, with trees and laughter, the story resumes itself in arctic regions among blinding snows. How can this be?
What began in the long and shining limousine seems closing now, fantastically, in a hansom cab.
The amorous business that ended with happiness forever after is starting all over again, this time with a curse and a pistol shot. It is not so good.

Nevertheless, though we know it all and cannot be fooled,
though we know the end and nothing deceives us,
Nevertheless we shall stay and see what it meant, the mystery
of the packed valise,
Why curses change at last to kisses and to laughter in a
limousine (for this is fixed, believe me, fixed),
How simply and how swiftly arctic blizzards melt into blowing trees and a village fair.

And stay to see the Hydra's head cut off, and grown again,
and incredibly multiplied,
And observe how Sisyphus fares when he has once more
almost reached the top,
How Tantalus again will nearly eat and drink.

And learn how Alph the sacred river flows, in Xanadu, forever to a sunless sea,
How, from the robes of simple flesh, fate emerges from new
and always more fantastic fate.

Until again we have the village scene. (And now we know
the meaning of the packed valise)
And it is a carnival again. In spring.

ART REVIEW

Recently displayed at the Times Square station, a new Vandyke on the face-cream girl.
(Artist unknown. Has promise, but lacks the brilliance shown by the great masters of the Elevated age)
The latest wood carving in a Whelan telephone booth, titled "O Mortal Fools WA 9-5090," shows two winged hearts above an ace of spades.
(His meaning is not entirely clear, but this man will go far)
A charcoal nude in the rear of Flatbush Ahearn's Bar & Grill, "Forward to the Brotherhood of Man," has been boldly conceived in the great tradition.
(We need more, much more of this)
Then there is the chalk portrait, on the walls of a waterfront warehouse, of a gentleman wearing a derby hat: "Bleecker Street Mike is a doublecrossing rat."
(Morbid, but powerful. Don't miss)

Know then by these presents, know all men by these signs and omens, by these simple thumbprints on the throat of time,
Know that Pete, the people's artist, is ever watchful,
That Tuxedo Jim has passed among us, and was much displeased, as always,
That George the Ghost (no man has ever seen him) and

Billy the Bicep boy will neither bend nor break,
That Mr. Harkness of Sunnyside still hopes for the best, and has not lost his human touch,
That Phantom Phil, the master of them all, has come and gone, but will return, and all is well.

CRACKED RECORD BLUES

If you watch it long enough you can see the clock move,
If you try hard enough you can hold a little water in the palm of your hand,
If you listen once or twice you know it's not the needle, or the tune, but a crack in the record when sometimes a phonograph falters and repeats, and repeats, and repeats, and repeats—

And if you think about it long enough, long enough, long enough, long enough then everything is simple and you can understand the times,
You can see for yourself that the Hudson still flows, that the seasons change as ever, that love is always love,
Words still have a meaning, still clear and still the same;
You can count upon your fingers that two plus two still equals, still equals, still equals, still equals—
There is nothing in this world that should bother the mind.

Because the mind is a common sense affair filled with common sense answers to common sense facts,
It can add up, can add up, can add up, can add up earthquakes and subtract them from fires,
It can bisect an atom or analyze the planets—
All it has to do is to, do is to, do is to, do is to start at the beginning and continue to the end.

STATISTICS

Sixty souls, this day, will arrange for travel to brighter lands
and bluer skies.
At sunset, two thousand will stop for a moment to watch
birds flying south.
In five thousand rooms the shades will be drawn, with the
lamps adjusted, the tables prepared, and the cards
arranged for solitaire.
This day, ninety-four will divorce, while thirty-three persons
meet great, though unexpected, financial success.
Twenty-one, on this day, will elect to die.

These are the figures, incontrovertibly; such are the facts.
Sixty, two thousand, five thousand, ninety-four, thirty-three,
twenty-one.

Actuary of actuaries, when these ordained numbers shall have
been fulfilled at the scheduled hour,
What shall be done to prove and redeem them, to explain
and preserve them?
How shall these accounts be balanced, otherwise than in per-
sonal flesh and blood?

By cold addition or subtraction? And on what fiery comp-
tometer?
Because the need for an answer that is correct is very great.

TRAVELOGUE IN A SHOOTING-GALLERY

There is a jungle, there is a jungle, there is a vast, vivid, wild, wild, marvelous, marvelous, marvelous jungle,
Open to the public during business hours,
A jungle not very far from an Automat, between a hat store there, and a radio shop.

There, there, whether it rains, or it snows, or it shines,
Under the hot, blazing, cloudless, tropical neon skies that the management always arranges there,
Rows and rows of marching ducks, dozens and dozens and dozens of ducks, move steadily along on smoothly-oiled ballbearing feet,
Ducks as big as telephone books, slow and fearless and out of this world,
While lines and lines of lions, lions, rabbits, panthers, elephants, crocodiles, zebras, apes,
Filled with jungle hunger and jungle rage and jungle love,
Stalk their prey on endless, endless rotary belts through never-ending forests, and burning deserts, and limitless veldts,
To the sound of tom-toms, equipped with silencers, beaten by thousands of savages hidden there.

And there it is that all the big game hunters go, there the

traders and the explorers come,
Leanfaced men with windswept eyes who arrive by streetcar, auto or subway, taxi or on foot, streetcar or bus,
And they nod, and they say, and they need no more:
"There . . . there . . .
There they come, and there they go."

And weighing machines, in this civilized jungle, will read your soul like an open book, for a penny at a time, and tell you all,
There, there, where smoking is permitted,
In a jungle that lies, like a rainbow's end, at the very end of every trail,
There, in the only jungle in the whole wide world where ducks are waiting for streetcars,
And hunters can be psychoanalyzed, while they smoke and wait for ducks.

THIRTEEN O'CLOCK

Why do they whistle so loud, when they walk past the graveyard late at night?
Why do they look behind them when they reach the gates? Why do they have any gates? Why don't they go through the wall?
But why, O why do they make that horrible whistling sound?

GO AWAY, LIVE PEOPLE, STOP HAUNTING THE DEAD.

If they catch you, it is said, they make you rap, rap, rap on a table all night,
And blow through a trumpet and float around the room in long white veils,
While they ask you, and ask you: Can you hear us, Uncle Ted?
Are you happy, Uncle Ted? Should we buy or should we sell? Should we marry, Uncle Ted?
What became of Uncle Ned, Uncle Ted, and is he happy, and ask him if he knows what became of Uncle Fred?

KEEP AWAY, LIVE PEOPLE, KEEP FAR AWAY,
STAY IN THE WORLD'S OTHER WORLD WHERE YOU REALLY BELONG, YOU WILL PROBABLY BE MUCH HAPPIER THERE.

And who knows what they are hunting for, always looking,
looking, looking with sharp bright eyes where they
ought to have sockets?
Whoever saw them really grin with their teeth?
Who knows why they worry, or what they scheme, with a
brain where there should be nothing but good,
damp air?

STAY AWAY, LIVE PEOPLE, STAY AWAY, STAY AWAY,
YOU MEAN NO HARM, AND WE AREN'T AFRAID OF YOU, AND WE
DON'T BELIEVE SUCH PEOPLE EXIST,
BUT WHAT ARE YOU LOOKING FOR? WHO DO YOU WANT?
WHO? WHO? WHO? O WHO?

CERTIFIED LIFE

The neighborhood athlete is in love again, staring about him with sightless eyes, and that, for him, is the same as having a patent on life;
The corner druggist can judge a person by his face, a talent as good as smuggled jewels, and that fixes everything, or nearly everything, for him;
Corporal Towne believes that he believes in Fate, a partnership Fate has never denied, and that takes care of Corporal Towne;
End problems in chess absorb the postman, and in this way he is taken care of, too—

And so, in some way, all people everywhere, all, all, all of us have our special but adequate arrangements made,
We hold the right tickets to the right destinations,
Have extra button which we use, when we must, to cloak us more tightly against the heavier storms,
Own magic lamps that we rub to change the darkest night into sunrise and then to perpetual noon,
Go everywhere with confidence, knowing our passports have been visa'd by a certain influential friend we happen to have in heaven—

And no man on earth, given three wishes, could possibly be

at a loss for his first, or second, or final wish;
There is no man whose papers, even for an hour, have not
been completely in order;
No one has ever forgotten the password, or totally lost his
ticket;
Or arrived at the familiar address of an ancient firm, to find
it no longer in business, and only vaguely known;
No one, no one ever waits for a bus, long after midnight, on
a rainy corner where the busline does not run at all.

RECEPTION GOOD

Now, at a particular spot on the radio dial, "—in this corner, wearing purple trunks,"
Mingles, somehow, with the news that "—powerful enemy units have been surrounded in the drive—"
And both of these with the information that "—there is a way to avoid having chapped and roughened hands."

Such are the new and complex harmonies, it seems, of a strange and still more complex age;
It is not that the reception is confused or poor, but rather it is altogether too clear and good,

And no worse, in any case, than that other receiving set, the mind,
Forever faithfully transmitting the great and little impulses that arrive, however wavering or loud, from near and far:
"It is an ill wind—" it is apt to report, underscoring this with "—the bigger they are the harder they fall," and simultaneously reminding, darkly, that "Things are seldom as they seem,"

Reconciling, with ease, the irreconcilable,

Piecing together fragments of a flashing past with clouded snapshots of the present and the future,
("Something old, something new," its irrelevant announcer states. "Something borrowed, something blue.")

Fashioning a raw, wild symphony of a wedding march, a drinking song, and a dirge,
Multiplying enormous figures with precision, then raising the question: But after all, what is a man?
Somehow creating hope and fresh courage out of ancient doubt.

"Both boys are on their feet, they're going to it," the radio reports,
"—the sinking was attended by a heavy loss of life—"
"—this amazing cream for quick, miraculous results."

How many pieces are there, in a simple jigsaw puzzle?
How many phases of a man's life can crowd their way into a single moment?
How many angels, actually, can dance on the point of a pin?

CONFESSION OVERHEARD IN A SUBWAY

You will ask how I came to be eavesdropping, in the first place.
The answer is, I was not.
The man who confessed to these several crimes (call him John Doe) spoke into my right ear on a crowded subway train, while the man whom he addressed (call him Richard Roe) stood at my left.
Thus, I stood between them, and they talked, or sometimes shouted, quite literally straight through me.
How could I help but overhear?
Perhaps I might have moved away to some other strap. But the aisles were full.
Besides, I felt, for some reason, curious.

"I do not deny my guilt," said John Doe. "My own, first, and after that my guilty knowledge of still further guilt.
I have counterfeited often, and successfully.
I have been guilty of ignorance, and talking with conviction. Of intolerable wisdom, and keeping silent.
Through carelessness, or cowardice, I have shortened the lives of better men. And the name for that is murder.
All my life I have been a receiver of stolen goods."

"Personally, I always mind my own business," said Richard Roe. "Sensible people don't get into those scrapes."

I was not the only one who overheard this confession.
Several businessmen, bound for home, and housewives and mechanics, were within easy earshot.
A policeman sitting in front of us did not lift his eyes, at the mention of murder, from his paper.
Why should I be the one to report these crimes?
You will understand why this letter to your paper is anonymous. I will sign it: Public Spirited Citizen, and hope that it cannot be traced.
But all the evidence, if there is any clamor for it, can be substantiated.
I have heard the same confession many times since, in different places.
And now that I think of it, I had heard it many times before.

"Guilt," said John, "is always and everywhere nothing less than guilt.
I have always, at all times, been a willing accomplice of the crass and the crude.
I have overheard, daily, the smallest details of conspiracies against the human race, vast in their ultimate scope, and conspired, daily, to launch my own.
You have heard of innocent men who died in the chair. It was my greed that threw the switch.
I helped, and I do not deny it, to nail that guy to the cross, and shall continue to help.
Look into my eyes, you can see the guilt.
Look at my face, my hair, my very clothing, you will see guilt written plainly everywhere.
Guilt of the flesh. Of the soul. Of laughing, when others do

not. Of breathing and eating and sleeping.
I am guilty of what? Of guilt. Guilty of guilt, that is all, and enough."

Richard Roe looked at his wristwatch and said: "We'll be twenty minutes late.
After dinner we might take in a show."

Now, who will bring John Doe to justice for his measureless crimes?
I do not, personally, wish to be involved.
Such nakedness of the soul belongs in some other province, probably the executioner's.
And who will bring the blunt and upright Richard Roe to the accuser's stand, where he belongs?
Or will he deny and deny his partnership?

I have done my duty, as a public spirited citizen, in any case.

SUBURBAN SUNSET, PRE-WAR, OR WHAT ARE WE MISSING?

These models (they were the very last word) arrived in the morning.
(The stock jobs came in three sizes: Small, medium, and rather huge)
Throughout breakfast, they absorbed every child in the village.
By noon, the wives and widows of the county declared themselves ravished.
Then in the evening the gentlemen returned from the city, to digest this affair. And were, in their turn, consumed.

Perhaps, to give a clearer picture of what transpired, one should describe a single, typical case.
Mr. Hone (his was the medium, in robin's egg blue) plugged in as directed and gave it the juice.
When nothing went, except a hissing from the tank of Just-right Air, he shook the cabinet, reread the instructions, then called Mr. Ballard of Mountain View Road.
Trying again with the lever at Maximum Force he turned on the current and stood back to watch.

Newark came in, and two city stations, but without much volume. And with none of the advertised results at all.

Mr. Hone then kicked the model (about where the knees would be) and threw a book-end at the instrument panel.

Still nothing. Nothing but an oblong stare from the shatter-proof full-view lens.

Swearing, Mr. Hone retired to the kitchen, made himself a highball, went out to the porch and stretched full length in a steamer chair.

Well, Mrs. Hone pointed out, he was perspiring freely, just as the company claimed he would be.

And his mind was fully occupied, exactly as guaranteed.

Nevertheless, night descended upon the county about as always.

Fragrantly. As damply as ever, but no damper. Neither more nor less quiet than the evening before.

KING JUKE

The juke-box has a big square face,
A majestic face, softly glowing with red and green and purple
lights.
Have you got a face as bright as that?

BUT IT'S A PROVEN FACT, THAT A JUKE-BOX HAS NO EARS.

With its throat of brass, the juke-box eats live nickels raw;
It can turn itself on or shut itself off;
It has no hangovers, knows no regrets, and it never feels the
need for sleep.
Can you do that?
What can you do that a juke-box can't, and do it ten times
better than you?

And it hammers at your nerves, and stabs you through the
heart, and beats upon your soul—
But can you do that to the box?

Its resourceful mind, filled with thoughts that range from
love to grief, from the gutter to the stars, from pole
to pole,
Can seize its thoughts between fingers of steel,
Begin them at the start and follow them through in an or-

derly fashion to the very end.
Can you do that?
And what can you say that a juke-box can't, and say it in a
clearer, louder voice than yours?
What have you got, a juke-box hasn't got?

Well, a juke-box has no ears, they say.
The box, it is believed, cannot even hear itself.
IT SIMPLY HAS NO EARS AT ALL.

BEWARE

Someone, somewhere, is always starting trouble,
Either a relative, or a drunken friend, or a foreign state.
Trouble it is, trouble it was, trouble it will always be.
Nobody ever leaves well enough alone.

It begins, as a rule, with an innocent face and a trivial re-
mark:
"There are two sides to every question," or "Sign right here,
on the dotted line,"
But it always ends with a crash of glass and a terrible shout—
No one, no one lets sleeping dragons sleep.

And it never happens, when the doorbell rings, that you find
a troupe of houris standing on your stoop.
Just the reverse.
So beware of doorbells. (And beware, beware of houris, too)
And you never receive a letter that says: "We enclose, here-
with, our check for a million."
You know what the letter always says, instead.
So beware of letters. (And anyway, they say, beware of great
wealth)

Be careful of doorbells, be cautious of telephones, watch out
for genial strangers, and for ancient friends;
Beware of dotted lines, and mellow cocktails; don't touch let-

ters sent specifically to you;
Beware, especially, of innocent remarks;
Beware of everything,
Damn near anything leads to trouble,
Someone is always, always stepping out of line.

ELEGY IN A THEATRICAL WAREHOUSE

They have laid the penthouse scenes away, after a truly phenomenal run,
And taken apart the courtroom, and the bright, shiny office, and laid them all away with the cabin in the clearing where the sun slowly rose through a smashing third act,
And the old family mansion on the road above the mill has been gone a long time,
And the road is gone—
The road that never did lead to any mill at all.

The telephone is gone, the phone that rang and rang, and never did connect with any other phone,
And the great steel safe where no diamonds ever were,
They have taken down the pictures, portraits of ancestors lost and unclaimed, that hung on the massive walls,
And taken away the books that reached to the study ceiling,
The rows and rows of books bound in leather and gold with nothing, nothing, nothing inside—

And the bureaus, and the chests, that were empty to the brim,
And the pistols that brought down so many, many curtains with so many, many blanks—

Almost everything is gone,
Everything that never held a single thing at all.

PIANO TUNER

It is the sound of a cat like no cat ever seen before walking
back and forth on ivory keys;
No note on this board, however the wires are tightened, can
be tuned to any other note;
The instrument cannot be played, not correctly,
Not by any players known today, not from the scores and
arrangements that now exist—

Somehow this wire, however strung, always returns a sound
with an overtone, and always in the overtone the
sound of distant gunfire can be plainly heard,
Another, however loose or taut, echoes as though to fingers
tapping not music but bulletins despatched from
remote time and space,
Then there are chords, neither minor chords nor discords, in
some way filled with a major silence—

And it cannot be, it is not according to the standard scale;
Some wholly new and different kind of scale, perhaps, with
unknown values, or no values, or values measured
by chance and change—

This key responds with something not even sound at all,
sometimes a feeling, and the feeling is anguish,

Sometimes a sense, like the touch of a hand,
Or a glimpse of familiar rooftops wrapped first in summer
sunlight and then in falling snow—

As though the instrument were devil'd by melodies not written yet,
Or possessed by players not yet born.

MODEL FOR A BIOGRAPHY

Years in sporting goods, rich in experience, were followed by
years in soda, candy, and cigars.
(If there is some connection, you might point it out here)
A real estate venture, resulting in ruin, prepared this man for
his later triumph in the hardware game.
(If there is no connection, or if the logic seems weak, his is
not the first life that failed to make sense—
You had better play it safe, and stick to one point):

HE WAS EXPERIENCED. HE WAS PREPARED.

And years of marriage (a happy, happy marriage) prepared
him for years and years of divorce.
(O happy divorce)
(But you'd better not say that. Think of the relatives. And
the public, by and large, would not believe you, or
if they did, would not understand)
Then what can you say? You have to say something that
makes a little sense:

HE WAS EXPERIENCED. HE WAS PREPARED.

He was kind, without fail, to other people's mothers;
Reprieved from insurance, he was sentenced to a bank, but

made a daring, spectacular daylight escape;
Rejected by the Marines, he was welcomed by the Quartermaster Corps with open arms,
And when it is over, well, when it is over:

HE WILL BE EXPERIENCED. HE WILL BE PREPARED.

END OF THE SEER'S CONVENTION

We were walking and talking on the roof of the world,
In an age that seemed, at that time, an extremely modern age
Considering a merger, last on the agenda, of the Seven Great Leagues that held the Seven True Keys to the Seven Ultimate Spheres of all moral, financial, and occult life.

"I foresee a day," said one of the delegates, an astro-analyst from Idaho, "when men will fly through the air, and talk across space;
They will sail in ships that float beneath the water;
They will emanate shadows of themselves upon a screen, and the shadows will move, and talk, and seem as though real."

"Very interesting, indeed," declared a Gypsy delegate.
"But I should like to ask, as a simple reader of tea-leaves and palms:
How does this combat the widespread and growing evil of the police?"

The astrologer shrugged, and an accidental meteor fell from his robes and smoldered on the floor.

"In addition," he said, "I foresee a war,
And a victory after that one, and after the victory, a war again."

"Trite," was the comment of a crystal-gazer from Miami Beach.
"Any damn fool, at any damn time, can visualize wars, and more wars, and famines and plagues.
The real question is: How to seize power from entrenched and organized men of Common Sense?"

"I foresee a day," said the Idaho astrologer, "when human beings will live on top of flag-poles,
And dance, at some profit, for weeks and months without any rest,
And some will die very happily of eating watermelons, and nails, and cherry pies."

"Why," said a bored numerologist, reaching for his hat, "can't these star-gazers keep their feet on the ground?"
"Even if it's true," said a Bombay illusionist, "it is not, like the rope-trick, altogether practical."

"And furthermore, and finally," shouted the astrologer, with comets and halfmoons dropping from his pockets, and his agitated sleeves,
"I prophesy an age of triumph for laziness and sleep, and dreams and utter peace.
I can see couples walking through the public parks in love, and those who do not are wanted by the sheriff.
I see men fishing beside quiet streams, and those who do not are pursued by collectors, and plastered with liens."

"This does not tell us how to fight against skepticism," muttered a puzzled mesmerist, groping for the door.
"I think," agreed a lady who interpreted the cards, "we are all inclined to accept too much on faith."

A sprinkling of rain, or dragon's blood,
Or a handful of cinders fell on the small, black umbrellas they raised against the sky.

FINALE

How cold, how very cold is the wind that blows out of nowhere into nowhere,
Winding across space and uncalendar'd time,

Filled with the sound of living voices, as it winds through
the ears that once were Stephen's ears,
Charged with the scent of fields and forests, as it blows
through the nostrils that once were Jane's,

Winding through the sockets that once were David's eyes,
Weaving again, as she used to do, the soft brown hair that
once was Mary's hair,
Bringing again the words that once were Stephen's and
David's and Mary's words into and out of their deaf
ears,
Scattering the worlds that once were theirs, and yours, and
mine,
Bearing away to nowhere and to no place the very especial
sins and virtues that once were ours,

How cold, how extremely cold is this wind.

THE JOYS OF BEING A BUSINESSMAN

Enter the proprietor of the Riviera Cafe;
Remarks, "It is a wonderful morning," as in fact it always is, for him;
Glances at the cash-register with marked disinterest, first, then at the morning man behind the bar, and at the early customers in front;
Disappears into the kitchen and at once returns, hangs up his coat;
Straightens the service flag in the window, and tests a Venetian blind;
States: "I was looking at the bills since ten o'clock, already;" (it is now about 11 A.M.)
Picks up a frond of palm leaves from the vase inside the door and inspects the stem, the leaves, the veins of the leaves;
Drinks coffee at the bar, peering steadily through the window at the street;
Queries, "Joe been here, yet?" And listens to the answer, Joe has not.

Puts on his coat and departs for a shave, returns, hangs up his coat;
Asserts: "Hot today. Another scorcher."

Studies the menu, frowns, shrugs in executive resignation, and
puts it down; no comment;
Has a glass of vermouth on the stroke of noon.

Declares: "Tell Joe I'll be back tonight," and puts on his coat;
Gives a final, disapproving survey, filled with the cares of the
High Command;
Austerely, but forgivingly departs.

PUBLIC LIFE

Then enter again, through a strange door, into a life again all
strange,
Enter as a rich man, or perhaps a poor man,
Enter as beggarman or thief, doctor or lawyer or merchant
or chief,
Enter, smiling, enter on tiptoe, enter blowing kisses, enter
in tears,

But enter, enter,
Enter in overalls, mittens, sweater and cap, grime and grit
and grease and gear,
Exit, then, exit and change, quick change and return,
Return in spats and pinstripe trousers, white bow tie and
high silk hat, studs and tails,

Return as the villain: "The mortgage is due." (A role you
never thought would be yours)
Enter as Nell (this comes with a shock): "You cur, you
fiend."
Enter the hero: "Gold is your God and may he serve you
well." (Can it possibly be this is you again?)

Enter Pa and Ma, strangers, stragglers, a miscellaneous crowd.
Enter Jane disguised as Du Barry, exit Du Barry disguised as
Jane,

Come in with gun and mask and murderous intent,
Leave with bloodless hands and a silent prayer, in peace,

Exit to thunder and lightning and clouds and the night,
Enter on the following morning in sunshine, to the sound
of birds,

Enter again to a different scene,
Enter again, through a strange door, into a life again all new
and strange.

A TRIBUTE, AND A NIGHTMARE

You wonder, sometimes, but more often worry, and feel dismayed in a world of change,
Seeing landmarks vanish, old bastions fall, and you frequently question what Fate may have in store for you—
But you really need not—
Whatever else it holds, it holds the changeless and eternal Martin Dies.

Will the world be bright, and filled with laughter?
You will hear all about it from Congressman Dies (Chairman of the Committee to Investigate Gloom).

Will the world be grim, inhabited by wolves with long, sharp teeth?
It will not go unchampioned. See Martin Dies, President of the Anti-Grandma League.

Will the people of the earth be nudists, eventually, and largely vegetarian?
Be especially wary of Dies, Martin, spinach crusader, the Kiddies' Kandidate unanimously acclaimed by Martin Dies.
Will the planet be Red with revolution (you hope) from the tropics to the poles?

You will have to deal (you fear, and rightly) with Commissar
Dies, Chairman of the Committee to Probe Versive
Activity.

Stranger, whoever you are, and whatever your final destination may be,
I give you, freely, a name to conjure with:
In heaven: Martin Dies, Chairman of the Membership Committee,
In hell: Martin Dies, President of United Coke & Coal.

AFTERNOON OF A PAWNBROKER

Still they bring me diamonds, diamonds, always diamonds,
Why don't they pledge something else for a change, if they must have loans, other than those diamond clasps and diamond rings,
Rubies, sapphires, emeralds, pearls,
Ermine wraps, silks and satins, solid gold watches and silver plate and violins two hundred years old,
And then again diamonds, diamonds, the neighborhood diamonds I have seen so many times before, and shall see so many times again?

Still I remember the strange afternoon (it was a season of extraordinary days and nights) when the first of the strange customers appeared,
And he waited, politely, while Mrs. Nunzio redeemed her furs, then he stepped to the counter and he laid down a thing that looked like a trumpet,
In fact, it was a trumpet, not mounted with diamonds, not plated with gold or even silver, and I started to say: "We can't use trumpets—"
But a light was in his eyes,
And after he was gone, I had the trumpet. And I stored it away. And the name on my books was Gabriel.

It should be made clear my accounts are always open to the police, I have nothing to conceal,
I belong, myself, to the Sounder Business Principles League,
Have two married daughters, one of them in Brooklyn, the other in Cleveland,
And nothing like this had ever happened before.
How can I account for my lapse of mind?
All I can say is, it did not seem strange. Not at the time. Not in that neighborhood. And not in that year.

And the next to appear was a man with a soft, persuasive voice,
And a kindly face, and the most honest eyes I have ever seen, and ears like arrows, and a pointed beard,
And what he said, after Mrs. Case had pledged her diamond ring and gone, I cannot now entirely recall,
But when he went away I found I had an apple. An apple, just an apple.
"It's been bitten," I remember that I tried to argue. But he smiled, and said in his quiet voice: "Yes, but only once."
And the strangest thing is, it did not seem strange. Not strange at all.

And still those names are on my books.
And still I see listed, side by side, those incongruous, and not very sound securities:
(1) Aladdin's lamp (I must have been mad), (1) Pandora's box, (1) Magic carpet,
(1) Fountain of youth (in good condition), (1) Holy Grail, (1) Invisible man (the only article never redeemed, and I cannot locate him), and others, others, many others,

And still I recall how my storage vaults hummed and crackled, from time to time, or sounded with music, or shot forth flame,
And I wonder, still, that the season did not seem one of unusual wonder, not even different—not at the time.

And still I think, at intervals, why didn't I, when the chance was mine, drink just once from that Fountain of youth?
Why didn't I open that box of Pandora?
And what if Mr. Gabriel, who redeemed his pledge and went away, should some day decide to blow on his trumpet?
Just one short blast, in the middle of some busy afternoon?

But here comes Mr. Barrington, to pawn his Stradivarius.
And here comes Mrs. Case, to redeem her diamond ring.